Celebrate the Months
JANUARY

EDITOR:
Kristine Johnson

ILLUSTRATORS:
Darcy Tom
Jana Travers
Jane Yamada

PROJECT DIRECTOR:
Carolea Williams

CONTRIBUTING WRITERS:
Joellyn Cicciarelli
Kimberly Jordano
Joel Kupperstein
Mary Kurth

TABLE OF CONTENTS

INTRODUCTION

Seasons, holidays, annual events, and just-for-fun monthly themes provide fitting frameworks for learning! Celebrate January and its special days with these exciting and unique activities. This activity book of integrated curriculum ideas includes the following:

MONTHLY CELEBRATION THEMES

▲ **monthly celebration activities** that relate to monthlong events or themes, such as Snowy Days, Chinese New Year, and Thank-You Month.

▲ **literature lists** of fiction and nonfiction books for each monthly celebration.

▲ **bulletin-board displays** that can be used for seasonal decoration and interactive learning-center fun.

▲ **take-home activities** that reinforce what is being taught in school, encourage home–school communication, and help children connect home and school learning.

SPECIAL-DAY THEMES

▲ **special-day activities** that relate to 15 special January days, including New Year's Day, Martin Luther King, Jr., Day, and Winnie-the-Pooh Day. Activities integrate art, language arts, math, science, and social studies.

▲ **calendar cards** that complement each of the 15 special days and add some extra seasonal fun to your daily calendar time.

▲ **literature lists** of fiction and nonfiction books for each special day.

FUN FORMS

▲ a **blank monthly calendar** for writing lesson plans, dates to remember, special events, book titles, new words, and incentives, or for math and calendar activities.

▲ **seasonal border pages** that add eye-catching appeal to parent notes, homework assignments, letters, certificates, announcements, and bulletins.

▲ **seasonal journal pages** for students to share thoughts, feelings, stories, or experiences. Reproduce and bind several pages for individual journals, or combine single, completed journal pages to make a class book.

▲ a **classroom newsletter** for students to report current classroom events and share illustrations, comics, stories, or poems. Reproduce and send completed newsletters home to keep families informed and involved.

▲ **clip art** to add a seasonal flair to bulletin boards, class projects, charts, and parent notes.

SPECIAL-DAY CALENDAR CARD ACTIVITIES

Below are a variety of ways to introduce special-day calendar cards into your curriculum.

PATTERNING

During daily calendar time, use one of these patterning activities to reinforce students' math skills.

▲ Use special-day calendar cards and your own calendar markers to create a pattern for the month, such as regular day, regular day, special day.

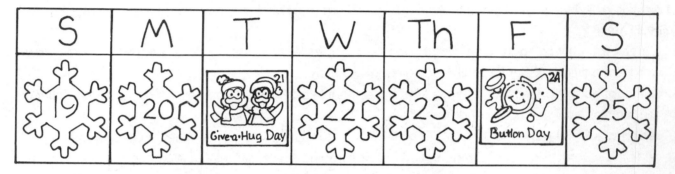

▲ Number special-day cards in advance. Use only even- or odd-numbered special days for patterning. (Create your own "special days" with the blank calendar cards.) Use your own calendar markers to create the other half of the pattern.

▲ At the beginning of the month, attach the special-day cards to the calendar. Use your own calendar markers for patterning. When a special day arrives, invite a student to remove the special-day card and replace it with your calendar marker to continue the pattern.

HIDE AND FIND

On the first day of the month, hide numbered special-day cards around the classroom. Invite students to find them and bring them to the calendar area. Have a student volunteer hang each card in the correct calendar space as you explain the card's significance.

A FESTIVE INTRODUCTION

On the first day of the month, display numbered special-day cards in a festive setting, such as a New Year's hat display. Invite students, one at a time, to remove a card and attach it to the calendar as you explain its significance.

POCKET CHART SENTENCE STRIPS

On the first day of the month, have the class dictate a sentence to correspond with each special-day card. For example, on Balloon Blast-Off Day you might write *On this special day, we make hot-air balloons.* Put the sentence strips away. When a special day arrives, place the corresponding strip in a pocket chart next to the calendar. Move a fun "pointer" (such as a balloon tied to a pencil) under the words, and have students read the sentence aloud. Add sentences to the pocket chart on each special day.

GUESS WHAT I HAVE

Discuss the special days and give each student a photocopy of one of the special-day cards. (Two or three students may have the same card.) Have students take turns describing their cards without revealing the special days, such as *This is the day we honor a man who made a speech called "I Have a Dream."* Invite the student who guesses Martin Luther King, Jr., Day to attach the card to the calendar.

TREAT BAGS

Place each special-day card and a small corresponding treat or prize in a resealable plastic bag. For example, place a honey packet in a bag for Winnie-the-Pooh Day. On the first day of the month, pin the bags on a bulletin board near the calendar. Remove the cards from the bags and attach them to the calendar as you discuss each day. As a special day arrives, remove the corresponding bag's contents and discuss them. Choose a student to keep the contents as a special reward.

LITERATURE MATCHUP

Have students sit in two lines facing each other. Provide the members of one group with special-day cards and the members of the other group with books whose subjects match the special-day cards held by the other group. Invite students to match cards and books, come forward in pairs, and introduce the day and book. Display the books near the calendar for students to read.

MINI-BOOKS

Reproduce numbered special-day cards so each student has a set. Have students sequence and staple their cards to make mini-books. Invite students to read their books and take them home to share with family members.

CREATIVE WRITING

Have each student glue a copy of a special-day card to a piece of construction paper. Invite students to illustrate and write about their special days. Have students share their writing. Display the writing near the calendar.

LUNCH SACK GAME

Provide each student with a paper lunch sack, a photocopy of each special-day card, and 15 index cards. Have students decorate the sacks for the month. Invite students to color the special-day cards and write on separate index cards a word or sentence describing each day. Have students place special-day cards and index cards in the sacks. Ask students to trade sacks, empty the contents, and match index cards to special-day cards.

SPECIAL-DAY BOX

One week before a special day, provide each student with a photocopied special-day card, an empty check box or shoe box, and a four-page square blank book. Ask each student to take the box, book, and card home to prepare a special-day box presentation. Have students write about the special day on the four book pages and place in the box small pictures or artifacts relating to the day. Ask students to decorate the boxes and glue their special-day cards to the top. Have students bring the completed boxes to school on the special day and give their presentations as an introduction to the day.

SNOWY DAYS

In many areas, January brings cold days filled with the fun of building snowmen, having snowball fights, and warming up with hot chocolate after a day of winter play. Share the fun and excitement of winter and the following "cool" activities, even if you live where winters are warm!

LITERATURE LINKS

The Big Snow
by Berta and Elmer Hader

Katie and the Big Snow
by Virginia Lee Burton

The Mitten
by Alvin Tresselt

Snowballs by Lois Ehlert

The Snowman
by Raymond Briggs

The Snowy Day
by Ezra Jack Keats

White Snow, Bright Snow
by Alvin Tresselt

Winter Rabbit
by Patrick Yee

FEED THE SNOWMAN BULLETIN BOARD

Cut two giant circles from white butcher paper to make a snowman. Cut a hole for the mouth in the top circle and a round hole in the second circle. Cover the second hole with clear plastic wrap. Attach the snowman to a blue background, stapling around the edges of the snowman and below the second hole. Have students decorate the snowman with a hat, scarf, and facial features. Invite students to paint white snowflakes on the background and attach paper snowflakes along the border. Display student work on the background. Have students "feed" the snowman with "snow" (paper squares) they earn for good conduct or finishing work. Reward the class when the snowman's belly is full.

MATERIALS
▲ white and blue butcher paper
▲ clear plastic wrap
▲ stapler
▲ hat
▲ scarf
▲ markers
▲ white paint/ paintbrushes
▲ paper snowflakes
▲ small white paper squares

SNOWMAN COUNTING BOOKS

MATERIALS

▲ Snowman reproducible (page 14)
▲ scissors
▲ glue
▲ orange foam board
▲ construction paper
▲ buttons
▲ markers
▲ stapler

Cut copies of the Snowman reproducible along the dotted lines, and give each student five copies. Have each student glue one foam-board nose to the first page, two construction-paper eyes to the second, three buttons to the third, and construction-paper mittens and boots, two each, to the fourth. Have students color five dots for a mouth on the last page. Ask students to complete the sentence frames by writing the number and names of items on the snowman. For example, on the first page students may write *I see <u>one orange nose</u> on my snowman*. Have students staple the pages inside a construction-paper cover. Invite students to draw a snowman on the inside back cover and glue all the items on him. Have them write *Now my snowman is alive!* Invite students to design a construction-paper snowman for the cover.

SNOW SCENES

MATERIALS

▲ 1 cup salt
▲ ½ cup flour
▲ ¾ cup water
▲ large bowl
▲ mixing spoon
▲ crayons
▲ light-blue construction paper
▲ paintbrushes

Make "snow" by mixing salt, flour, and water in a large bowl. Invite students to use crayons to draw a winter scene on light-blue construction paper. Have students paint "snow" over their pictures using long brush strokes. (Ask students to apply only a thin layer. The snow will not show up until the mixture has dried.)

MITTEN MATH

MATERIALS
▲ old mittens or construction-paper mittens
▲ chart paper

Collect an assortment of old mittens, or cut a variety of construction-paper mittens. Divide the class into small groups, and give each group a variety of mittens. Ask students to sort the mittens according to color, size, right and left hands, or patterns and solids. Invite students to arrange the mittens into a pattern such as red, blue, blue; red, blue, blue. Have one student from each group share a pattern. Then, have one student at a time lie on the floor while the other group members line up mittens from the heel to head. Graph the results on chart paper. Mittens can also be used for counting, adding, and subtracting activities.

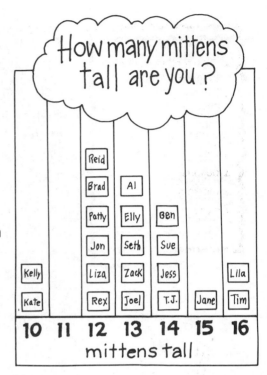

How many mittens tall are you?

10	11	12	13	14	15	16
		Reid				
	Brad	Al				
	Patty	Elly	Ben			
	Jon	Seth	Sue			
Kelly	Liza	Zack	Jess			Lila
Kate	Rex	Joel	T.J.	Jane	Tim	

mittens tall

SNOWBALL TOSS

MATERIALS
▲ masking tape
▲ newspaper
▲ 2 large trash cans
▲ timer

Divide the class into two groups. Push desks and chairs aside to create a large open space. Use masking tape to divide the room in half, with one team on each side of the tape. Provide each team with newspaper and a large trash can. Have teams crumple the newspaper into "snowballs." Challenge students to throw snowballs into the opposing team's trash can while on their knees. Set a timer for two minutes and say *Go*. When time is up, the team who has tossed the most snowballs in the other team's trash can wins. Have each team clean up the other team's side of the room.

MATERIALS
- ▲ 4 parts powdered laundry soap (not detergent)
- ▲ 1 part water
- ▲ hand mixer
- ▲ large bowl
- ▲ toothpicks
- ▲ small twigs
- ▲ decorations (cloves, candy corn, raisins, felt scraps)

SOAPY SNOWMEN

Whip soap and water in a large bowl until the mixture resembles dough. Give a small amount of dough to each student. Have students use their hands to shape the dough into three balls. Have them stack the three balls and connect them with toothpicks. Invite students to decorate their "snowmen" with twig arms, clove eyes, a candy-corn nose, raisin buttons, and a felt scarf. (As the soap dries, it will turn from gray to white.)

MATERIALS
- ▲ waxed paper
- ▲ snowflake pattern (page 96)
- ▲ glue guns
- ▲ glitter
- ▲ scissors
- ▲ white thread

LET IT SNOW, LET IT SNOW, LET IT SNOW

Invite students to create sparkly snowflakes. Have them place waxed paper over a copy of the snowflake pattern, trace the pattern with a glue gun, and sprinkle it with glitter. Let the snowflakes dry before cutting around the waxed paper. Tie thread through the snowflakes and hang them from the ceiling.

GLITTER

DOORSTOP SNOWMAN

To make a doorstop, first have students fill ³/₄ of a white sock with rice and wrap three rubber bands around it to make three sections. Ask students to fold over the top of the sock and wrap a colored sock over it as a floppy hat. Invite students to glue on a pom-pom nose, twist-tie mouth, felt scarf, wiggly eyes, and buttons, and have them stick in pipe-cleaner arms. Help students cut out tiny felt mittens to glue to the arms. Invite students to give their snowman doorstop to a family member.

SLUSHY SNOW TREATS

Give each student a cup and a resealable plastic bag with a few ice cubes. Invite students to smash their ice cubes with wooden blocks to make crushed ice. Supervise students and remind them of safe-handling practices. Invite students to carefully place the ice in their cups. Pour a few spoonfuls of fruit juice over the ice for a tasty treat.

SNOW PEOPLE

Have students cut two large construction-paper snowmen. Send them home for students to decorate with their families. Have students bring decorated snowmen back to school. Invite students to leave the bottom open when they staple the snowmen together, stuff the snowmen with crumpled newspaper or cotton balls, and staple the bottom. Hang the snowmen from the ceiling, and have students vote for awards in categories such as *Most Original, Most Realistic, Most Creative, Funniest,* or *Best Use of Materials.* Be sure each student receives an award.

I see _____

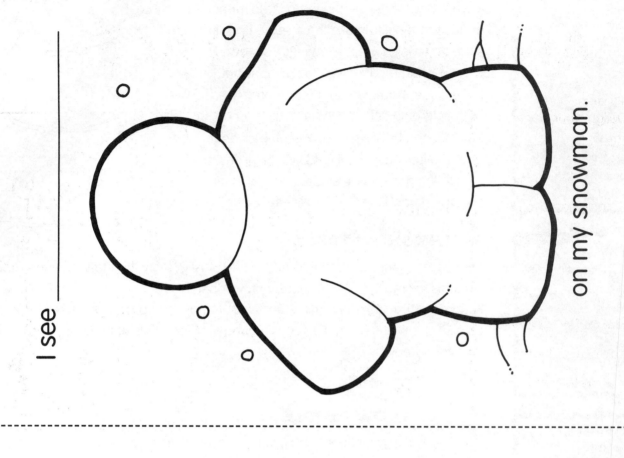

on my snowman.

- -

I see _____

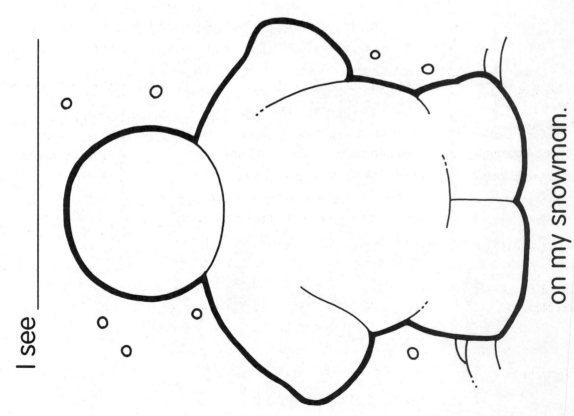

on my snowman.

January © 1997 Creative Teaching Press

PENGUINS, POLAR BEARS, AND ARCTIC PLACES

Delight your students during the chilly month of January with activities involving polar animals and places. Let students waddle like penguins and growl like polar bears as they dive into this "cool" theme!

LITERATURE LINKS

Cuddly Dudley
by Jez Alborough

Funny Feet! by Leatie Weiss

Little Penguin's Tale
by Audrey Wood

Little Polar Bear and the Brave Little Hare by Hans de Beer

Mama, Do You Love Me?
by Barbara M. Joosse

Penguins
by Bobbie Kalman

Tacky the Penguin
by Helen Lester

PENGUIN POWER BULLETIN BOARD

Read *Tacky the Penguin* aloud. Discuss how penguins are different from other birds. Ask students what makes Tacky unique. Have students share something that makes themselves unique and write about or draw it on speech bubbles. Invite students to cut and glue fabric scraps on the Penguin reproducible to design funky shirts like the one Tacky wears. Have students cut out their penguins. Display the penguins with the speech bubbles on a bulletin board titled *Penguin Power*.

MATERIALS
▲ *Tacky the Penguin* by Helen Lester
▲ speech bubbles
▲ scissors
▲ glue
▲ fabric scraps
▲ Penguin reproducible (page 21)

PENGUIN PEEK-OVER BOOKS

MATERIALS
- ▲ *Penguins*
  by Bobbie Kalman
- ▲ scissors
- ▲ Peek-Over reproducible
  (page 22)
- ▲ 3 ½" x 7 ½"
  (9 cm x 19 cm)
  writing paper
- ▲ stapler

Read *Penguins* aloud. Have students imagine they are penguins and write a description of a typical day. Ask students to cut on the dotted lines of the Peek-Over reproducible. Have students write final drafts on writing paper and staple sheets to the bottom portion. Have students fold the reproducible on the fold line so the bottom portion tucks under the penguin's chin and write a title on the front.

PRATTLING PENGUINS

MATERIALS
- ▲ drawing paper
- ▲ scissors
- ▲ crayons or markers
- ▲ glue

Penguins live in large colonies, called rookeries, where they make lots of noise. Invite students to make their own chatty penguins. Have each student fold a piece of paper in half like a card and, in the center of the fold, cut a 2 ½" (6 cm) line perpendicular to the fold. Have students form two triangle shapes in the paper by folding back each cut flap. Ask students to unfold the flaps, reach inside the card, and tuck the flaps inside the paper, creasing the fold line to form a V. Have students open their papers to form a pop-out mouth. Invite students to draw eyes above the mouth and a bow tie below. Have students draw a head and shoulders and color the penguin black and white. Have students write, cut out, and glue on speech bubbles to record their penguins' babbling.

PENGUIN SHUFFLE

Penguin parents help care for their eggs. They take turns cradling eggs on their feet. Invite students to test their balancing skills, penguin-style. Divide the class into two teams. Give each of the first players in line a beanbag "egg," and have them place it on their feet. Have students try to shuffle across the room and back without dropping their eggs. Have students pass the eggs to the next "penguins" in line and sit down. The first team to finish wins.

INDOOR IGLOO

Arctic natives call themselves *Inuit,* which means "the people." *Igloo* is the Inuit name for shelter. Igloos are often made of ice blocks. Have students make a class igloo from cardboard boxes. Ask students to paint the boxes white (or wrap them in white butcher paper). Tape all the boxes together. Include windows and a tunnel opening. Glue a construction-paper "fire" to the inside wall, and place arctic literature and throw pillows inside. Invite students to sit inside this cozy reading niche.

INKBLOT TOTEM POLES

Arctic natives make totem poles by carving animals, birds, and other forms of nature into wood. Distribute drawing paper for students to use in designing their own totem poles. Have each student fold the paper in half. Ask students to open their papers and drip spots of paint along the fold. Have students fold the paper, rub it, and open it to dry. When their papers are dry, students can cut out the shapes made by the blots, add details with markers, and glue the design onto paper-towel tubes to make totem poles.

POLAR POCKET-CHART RELAY

Cut out the questions and answers from the Polar Facts reproducible. Glue each answer to a large index card, and place the cards in the pocket chart, leaving the top row blank. Divide the class into two groups. Ask a question from the Polar Facts sheet. Invite one student from each group to find the right answer and move it to the top of the chart. The student who moves the correct card to the top asks a student from the other group to read the answer aloud. Continue asking polar questions until everyone plays.

SCRIMSHAW NECKLACES

Scrimshaw is the carving or engraving of objects made from teeth or bone. Arctic hunters carved tools and charms from walrus ivory and engraved them with animal images to bring good luck. To simulate scrimshaw, first drop globs of plaster or craft dough on waxed paper. Have students flatten the globs and make a hole at one edge with a pencil. After the plaster hardens or the dough is cooked, have students scratch designs with tacks or small nails. (Carefully supervise children using sharp objects, and remind them of safe-handling practices.) Have students apply black paint in the grooves to define their designs. Shellac their "scrimshaw" when dry. Invite students to thread yarn through the hole and wear their necklaces.

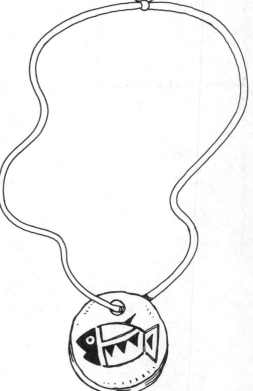

FISHY FRACTIONS

Divide the class into groups of four, and give each group four copies of the Penguin reproducible to be used as work mats and twelve fish-shaped crackers. To present the concepts of halves, thirds, and fourths, ask students to share the crackers evenly between two students, and then have them share the crackers among three and four students. Invite students to take turns telling fishy fraction story problems such as *There were three penguins who shared twelve fish. How many fish did each penguin get?*

DO YOU LOVE ME?

HOME ACTIVITY

Read the Inuit story *Mama, Do You Love Me?* to your class. Ask students to describe things they do that make them wonder if their family members still love them. Invite students to copy and complete the frame, _____, *do you love me when I* _____? on the Inuit reproducible and glue cotton balls around the face, cuffs, and waist. Send students' completed papers home along with a blank copy for family members to read and respond to. Have students cut out the Inuit figures and glue them back-to-back. Invite students to share what they discussed with their family members.

POLAR FACTS

▲ Do polar bears eat penguins?

No. Polar bears live in the Northern Hemisphere and penguins live in the Southern Hemisphere.

▲ What do polar bears eat?

They eat seals, seabirds, fish, grass, and berries.

▲ Why do polar bears stand on their rear legs?

They look around and sniff the air searching for food. They can smell a seal that's more than three miles (five km) away.

▲ Do polar bears live in the ocean?

No. They usually live on ice, but they can swim more than a hundred miles (160 km) without stopping to rest.

▲ What do penguins eat?

They eat fish, squid, and krill.

▲ Do penguins fly?

No, but they are still birds.

▲ Do penguins swim?

Yes, but they are not fish.

▲ Do penguins have feathers?

Yes. Their feathers are coated with oil that makes them waterproof.

▲ Do all penguins live in a cold climate?

No. Some live close to the equator and most migrate to warmer areas during the winter.

▲ Could you swim faster than a penguin?

No. Penguins normally swim around 15 miles (24 km) an hour, faster than any human swimmer.

▲ Why do penguins look like they are wearing tuxedos?

They have countershading (like killer whales) to help them blend with the dark ocean when seen from above and blend with the light sky when seen from below. Their colors also help them warm up or cool down, depending on whether they lie on their stomach or back.

Penguins, Polar Bears, and Arctic Places

January © 1997 Creative Teaching Press

PENGUIN

PEEK-OVER

- fold up -

INUIT

CHINESE NEW YEAR

Chinese New Year is an important Chinese holiday that falls between mid-January and mid-February. The actual day is determined by the Chinese lunar calendar. This holiday is a time to remember friends, ancestors, and family. *Gung Hay Fat Choy*— Happy New Year!

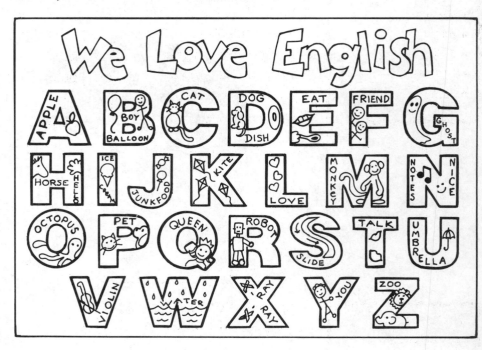

LITERATURE LINKS

China, the Culture by Bobbie Kalman

The Chinese New Year by Tricia Brown

Count Your Way through China by Jim Haskins

The Eyes of the Dragon by Margaret Leaf

Gung Hay Fat Choy: Happy New Year by June Behrens

I Hate English by Ellen Levine

The Last Dragon by Susan Miho Nunes

Lion Dancer by Kate Waters and Madeline Slovenz-Low

WE LOVE ENGLISH BULLETIN BOARD

In advance, draw individual block alphabet letters on tagboard and cut them out. Read aloud the story *I Hate English.* Distribute a tagboard letter to each student. (If you have more or less than 26 students, share letters or invite small groups to work on extra letters.) Have each student think of one or two words beginning with the letter that would be important for someone learning English to know and write them and illustrate them on the tagboard letter. Invite students to share their letters and important words with the class and tell why they think the words are important. Attach the letters to a bulletin board titled *We Love English.*

MATERIALS
▲ tagboard
▲ scissors
▲ *I Hate English* by Ellen Levine
▲ crayons or markers

MATERIALS

- ▲ 8" (20 cm) red construction-paper squares
- ▲ tape
- ▲ drawing paper
- ▲ crayons or markers
- ▲ scissors
- ▲ yarn
- ▲ glue
- ▲ construction paper
- ▲ bookbinding materials

LUCKY CLASS BOOK

Explain to students that during the Chinese New Year Chinese children receive red envelopes with gold coins inside for luck. Have each student fold three corners of a red construction-paper square into the center to make an envelope and tape the corners together. Invite each student to draw a picture of a gift they would give for good luck. Have each student cut out the "good luck charm" and tape it to a piece of yarn. Have students tape the other end of the yarn inside the envelope. Invite students to glue their envelopes to construction paper and put their charms inside. Have students write on the construction paper *I'm giving you _____ for good luck.* Bind papers into a class book titled *Our Lucky Book.* Invite students to read the pages and peek at the lucky items in the envelopes.

I'm giving you *a bunny* for good luck.

MATERIALS

- ▲ sturdy paper plates
- ▲ scissors
- ▲ tempera paint/ paintbrushes
- ▲ tape
- ▲ 7" (18 cm)-diameter pastel tissue-paper circles
- ▲ hole punch
- ▲ yarn
- ▲ dowel or stick
- ▲ tissue-paper streamers

LIGHT THE LANTERNS

The Chinese celebrate the new year with a Festival of Lanterns, during which children carry lanterns through the streets. Let students make lanterns for their own festival. Have each student cut out the center of three paper plates, paint the top side of each plate-ring, and let the plate-rings dry. Have each student tape a pastel tissue-paper circle to the back and hole-punch the top and sides of each plate (at 12, 3, and 9 o'clock). Have students tie the plates together with yarn at 3 and 9 o'clock and thread 12" (30.5 cm) of yarn through the top hole of each plate. Invite students to knot the yarn together at the top, tie the plates to a dowel or stick, and add tissue-paper streamers to the bottom.

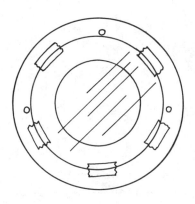

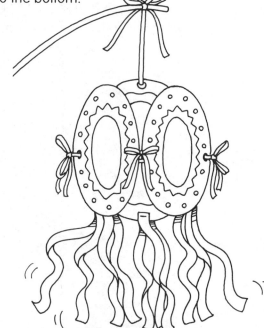

MATERIALS

- ▲ 12" x 18" (30.5 x 46 cm) green construction paper
- ▲ stapler
- ▲ glue
- ▲ scissors
- ▲ construction-paper scraps
- ▲ tinsel, glitter, and sequins

DRAGON HAT PARADE

In Chinese folklore, dragons are symbols of luck that bring rain, gifts, and peace. Give each student two sheets of green construction paper, stapled end to end to form one long sheet. Wrap the construction paper around each student's head, stapling the sides together about an inch or two (5–10 cm) from the child's forehead. Have students glue together the flaps that project from the brow band. Invite each student to cut triangle mouths and zigzag scales across the top and glue colorful construction-paper fringe to the chin. Have students add a construction-paper tongue and eyes. Invite students to use tinsel, glitter, and sequins to add sparkle to their dragons. On the first day of the Chinese New Year, have students wear their hats and parade from room to room.

MATERIALS

- ▲ dragon hat

CHASE THE DRAGON'S TAIL

Have students line up in groups of at least ten with the first student in line wearing a dragon hat. Ask students behind the "dragon" to put their hands on the shoulders of the person in front of them. Give the dragon one minute to try to tag the last child in line without causing the line to break apart. If the dragon succeeds, he or she wins; if the line breaks or the dragon does not tag the last child, he or she becomes the tail, and the next student in line wears the hat.

MATERIALS

▲ Chinese Calendar
reproducible (page 28)

▲ crayons or markers

▲ drawing paper

▲ bookbinding materials

YEAR OF THE . . .

Each year of the Chinese calendar is named after a different animal. There are twelve years in a cycle. Many Chinese believe that people born in the year of a certain animal exhibit particular characteristics. Have students find the animal for their birth year and complete the Chinese Calendar reproducible. Invite students to invent their own animals or imaginary creatures with character traits to illustrate on drawing paper. Bind the drawings into a class book.

MATERIALS

▲ Fortune Cookies
reproducible (page 29)

▲ ¹/₂" x 2 ¹/₂"
(1 cm x 7 cm)
paper strips

▲ resealable plastic
bags

FORTUNE COOKIES

Give each student a copy of the Fortune Cookies reproducible and twelve paper strips in a resealable plastic bag to take home. Invite families to create their own fortunes on the paper strips and bake cookies together. Invite each student to bring in one fortune cookie on a designated day to trade with a friend. (Prepare extra cookies for students who forget to bring them to class.)

CHINESE CALENDAR

Name _____

TIGER 1950, 1962, 1974, 1986, 1998 aggressive, courageous, sensitive	**HARE** 1951, 1963, 1975, 1987, 1999 affectionate, shy, talented	**DRAGON** 1952, 1964, 1976, 1988, 2000 complex, passionate, healthy	**SNAKE** 1953, 1965, 1977, 1989, 2001 wise, vain, hot-tempered
HORSE 1954, 1966, 1978, 1990, 2002 popular, attractive, impatient	**SHEEP** 1955, 1967, 1979, 1991, 2003 elegant, creative, timid	**MONKEY** 1956, 1968, 1980, 1992, 2004 intelligent, enthusiastic, discouraged	**ROOSTER** 1957, 1969, 1981, 1993, 2005 selfish, devoted, eccentric
DOG 1958, 1970, 1982, 1994, 2006 loyal, honest, stubborn	**BOAR** 1959, 1971, 1983, 1995, 2007 noble, chivalrous, friendly	**RAT** 1960, 1972, 1984, 1996, 2008 ambitious, honest, frivolous	**OX** 1961, 1973, 1985, 1997, 2009 bright, patient, inspiring

What is the animal name for your birth year? _____

How are you like that animal? _____

_____

How are you different from that animal? _____

_____

What are the animal names for your family members' birth years?

_____

January © 1997 Creative Teaching Press

FORTUNE COOKIES

Chinese fortune cookies are fun and easy to make. Children will especially enjoy making cookies with special fortunes written by family members. Begin by writing fortunes with your child on the pieces of paper. Then follow the recipe below.

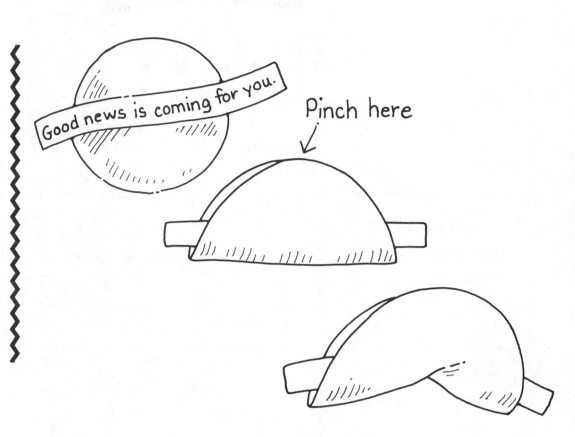

Good news is coming for you.

Pinch here

INGREDIENTS
- ▲ 1 large egg
- ▲ ¹/₄ cup sugar
- ▲ 2 tablespoons oil
- ▲ ¹/₄ cup cornstarch
- ▲ 2 tablespoons water

Directions

1. Mix the egg and sugar. When mixture is thick and smooth, mix in the oil.

2. Put the cornstarch in a small bowl. Add water and a small amount of the egg mixture. Stir until smooth.

3. Combine the cornstarch and egg mixtures, and beat them into a batter.

4. Drop heaping teaspoons of batter onto a hot, lightly greased griddle. Spread the drops until they are about 3" (7.5 cm) in diameter. They will look like very thin pancakes. Cook one side until light brown (about three minutes) and turn with a spatula. Cook about three more minutes and remove.

5. Quickly place a fortune in the center of each cookie and fold the cookies in half. Pinch the edges together.

6. Lightly bend the cookies in the middle.

(Makes one dozen.)

THANK-YOU MONTH

January 11th is International Thank-You Day, which makes January the perfect month to show appreciation for others. Devote some time this month to expressing gratitude through fun activities that focus on those two magic words—*thank you.*

LITERATURE LINKS

The Jolly Postman
by Janet & Allan Ahlberg

Kid's Address Book
by Michael Levine

Manners by Aliki

Soup Should Be Seen, Not Heard!
by Beth Brainard and Sue Behr

Special Delivery
by Betty Brandt

Thank-You Book
by Francoise Seignobosc

Thank You, You're Welcome
by Louis Slobodkin

What's for Lunch? by Eric Carle

CATCH THEM SAYING THANK YOU

Cut several brown baseball-mitt shapes and white baseball shapes from construction paper. Teach students how to say *thank you* in different languages. When you catch a student saying *thank you* in a foreign language, invite the student to write the new word in the baseball shape and draw or write on the mitt why he or she was saying thank you. Invite students to attach the mitts and balls to a bulletin board titled *I Caught You Saying Thank You!*

MATERIALS
▲ scissors
▲ brown and white construction paper

Spanish—*Gracias* (GRAH-see-us)
French—*Merci* (mehr-SEE)
German—*Danke* (DAHN-keh)
Italian—*Grazie* (GRAH-zee-ay)
Japanese—*Arigato* (ah-ree-GAH-toe)

Vietnamese—*Cám on* (KAM-ung)
Chinese—*Xìe xìe* (shay-shay)
Russian—*Sbasiba* (SPAHS-ee-bah)
Swahili—*Ahsante* (uh-SAHN-tay)
Korean—*Kum sa hum me da* (kuhm-saw-HUM-mee-dah)

THANKS FOR YOUR HELP

MATERIALS
- ▲ writing paper
- ▲ crayons or markers
- ▲ bookbinding materials

Invite students to write thank-you notes from the perspective of animals or inanimate objects. For example, students could write thank-you notes from pants to a belt, from feet to sneakers, from hands to mittens, from a bike to its tire, from a head to a helmet, or from a flea to a dog. Have students illustrate their notes. Then bind the notes into a class book titled *Thanks!*

I APPRECIATE YOU

MATERIALS
- ▲ Thank-You Notes reproducible (page 34)
- ▲ scissors

Give each student two or three copies of the Thank You Notes reproducible. Have students print a different student's name on each note and cut them apart. Ask students to write a thank-you message on each note and place it in each chosen student's desk, mailbox, or cubby.

COURTEOUS CONDUCT

MATERIALS
- ▲ fairy tale with impolite characters
- ▲ video camera
- ▲ videotape
- ▲ VCR

Read a fairy tale in which characters are particularly impolite, such as *The Three Little Pigs*. Invite students to act out a funny version of the story using polite words such as *please* and *thank you,* even when the characters are angry. Videotape the performance and play the tape for the class. Discuss how the tone and seriousness of the story changed when characters were polite. Explain that, just like in the play, it is hard to become upset when someone is polite.

GIVING THANKS AT HOME

Before Open House, invite students to think of one reason they are thankful for their parents. Record students one at a time on video- or audiotape giving thanks. Create a display area for the VCR or audiotape player with a sign that says *Thanks Mom and Dad!* Play the tape at Open House.

MATERIALS

▲ video camera or audiotape recorder
▲ video- or audiotape
▲ VCR or audiotape player

RAINBOW HANDS

Cover the work area with newspaper. Pour a different color of tempera paint on each of six paper plates. Have students wear smocks, and have one student at a time put a hand in the paint and press it onto the butcher paper. Begin with an arc of red, then orange, yellow, green, blue, and purple. Place a water bucket and towel nearby for students to rinse and dry their hands with. When dry, write *Thanks for making our world brighter!* across the rainbow. Have students sign their names. This makes a great gift for your school principal or a community helper.

MATERIALS

▲ newspaper
▲ 3' x 5' (2.5 m x 4.5 m) butcher paper
▲ 6 paper plates
▲ rainbow-colored tempera paint
▲ smocks
▲ water bucket
▲ old towel
▲ marker

PEEK-A-BOO THANK-YOUS

Have students fold construction paper in half to make a card. Have them fold the card front in half and cut a shape such as a heart, circle, or square on the fold creating a "window" to the inside. Invite students to draw a small picture on the inside so that it peeks through the front or cut a shape smaller than the window (from another piece of paper) and glue it to a piece of thread. Have students tape the thread inside and above the window, so the shape hangs in the window's center. Invite students to write a thank-you note to someone special.

2 example # 1

3 example # 2

I'M THANKFUL FOR MY CHILD

HOME ACTIVITY

Send home a copy of the reproducible from page 35 with each student. Invite parents to write why they are thankful for their child and return the paper to school. When all have been returned, read the papers aloud. Bind the papers in a class book. Be sure to display the book at Open House.

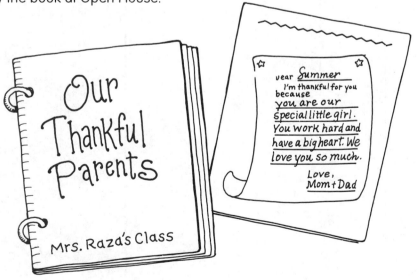

THANK-YOU NOTES

Thank you for

Thank you for

Thank you for

Thank you for

January © 1997 Creative Teaching Press

Dear_____,

I'm thankful for you because

_____

_____

_____

_____

_____

_____

Love,

_____

EYE HEALTH-CARE MONTH

January is National Eye Health-Care Month and a good time for students to learn more about their eyes and eye care. January 4 is the birthday of Louis Braille, who was blinded as a child and developed a system of raised dots representing letters of the alphabet to help blind people read. Give your students eye-opening experiences with these exciting activities!

LITERATURE LINKS

Arthur's Eyes by Marc Brown

Cromwell's Glasses by Holly Keller

Eyes by Judith Worthy

Fish Eyes by Lois Ehlert

Glasses: Who Needs 'Em? by Lane Smith

Look at Your Eyes by Paul Showers

Spectacles by Ellen Raskin

Willis by James Marshall

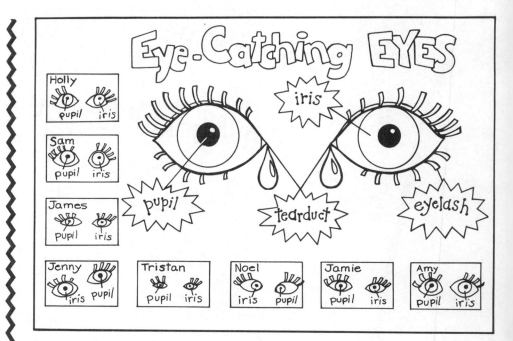

EYE-CATCHING BULLETIN BOARD

Paint large eyes in the center of a bulletin board display. Make three-dimensional eyelashes by cutting strips from black construction paper and curling them around a pencil. Cut foil in the shape of exaggerated tears and attach below tear ducts. Label eye parts *iris, eyelid, pupil, eyelash,* and *tear duct.* Invite students to paint eyes on drawing paper. When the eyes are dry, have students curl and glue on black construction-paper lashes and label eye parts. Display on a bulletin board titled *Eye-Catching Eyes.*

MATERIALS
- ▲ paint/paintbrushes
- ▲ butcher paper
- ▲ scissors
- ▲ black construction paper
- ▲ pencil
- ▲ foil
- ▲ glue
- ▲ drawing paper

APPLE-OF-MY-EYE CLASS BOOK

List the following eye expressions on chart paper. Without explaining their meanings, invite each student to illustrate a phrase on eye-shaped paper. Staple papers into a class book with an eye-shaped construction-paper cover. Read the book aloud and discuss the phrases' meanings.

MATERIALS
- ▲ chart paper
- ▲ crayons or markers
- ▲ eye-shaped drawing paper
- ▲ stapler
- ▲ eye-shaped construction paper

a nod's as good as a wink

an eye for an eye

apple of my eye

bird's-eye view

blink and you miss it

eagle eye

evil eye

eye contact

eye-opener

eyeball-to-eyeball

eyesore

forty winks

good eye

green-eyed monster

in the eye of the beholder

in the twinkle of an eye

it caught my eye

look straight in the eye

love is blind

out of sight

out of the corner of my eye

rose-colored glasses

EYE-COLOR GRAPH

MATERIALS
- ▲ small paper squares
- ▲ crayons or markers
- ▲ chart paper
- ▲ sentence strips

Have each student draw an eye on a paper square and color the iris to match his or her own. Label chart paper with eye colors for a class eye-color graph. Invite students to attach their drawings to the chart paper. Ask students questions such as *How many more brown-eyed students are there than blue-eyed students? How many students have hazel eyes? If each student has two eyes, how many green eyes are there in the class?* Write student observations on sentence strips and display them around the eye-color graph.

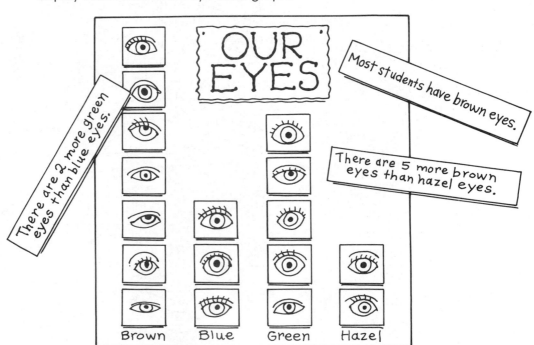

SOMEDAY I HOPE TO SEE . . .

Gather students in a circle. Hold up a pair of glasses and share some wonderful things you can see with your "magical" glasses. Ask students to share some marvelous things they would like to see with the glasses. Invite students to draw self-portraits and glue on magical pipe-cleaner glasses. Have students complete on speech bubbles the sentence *Someday I hope to see* _____. Invite students to glue speech bubbles on their self-portraits. Display them in the classroom.

ANIMAL EYES

Challenge students to identify animals by looking only at the animals' eyes. Cut out the eyes from animal pictures, and laminate the eyes and pictures. Have students try to match the animals' eyes with the pictures. Discuss unique animal-eye characteristics such as large pupils for seeing in the dark (cats) or eyes with special eyelids for seeing underwater (alligators). Place the eyes and pictures in a learning center.

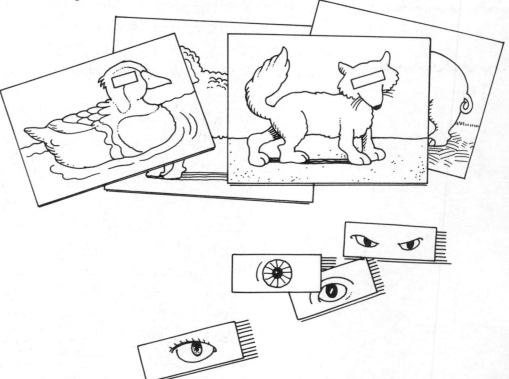

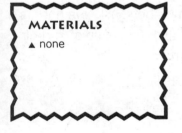

EYE EMOTIONS

MATERIALS
- ▲ *Cromwell's Glasses* by Holly Keller
- ▲ drawing paper
- ▲ crayons or markers
- ▲ art supplies (glue, scissors, egg cartons, yarn, toothpicks, milk caps)

Demonstrate different ways eyes show emotions—wide eyes show fear, rolled eyes show disbelief, and shifty eyes show sneakiness. Read *Cromwell's Glasses* to your class. As you read, have students use their eyes to show the different emotions Cromwell and his friends express. Have students draw their faces and use art supplies to show an emotion with their eyes. Invite students to share an experience they had that made them feel that emotion.

EYE TALK

MATERIALS
- ▲ index cards

Have each student write on an index card one question to ask an eye doctor before a visit, such as *How do we see? What do lashes do?* or *Why do we blink and cry?* Take a field trip to an eye clinic, or ask an ophthalmologist or optometrist to visit your classroom. Ask the doctor to discuss rules for eye care, sight aids such as glasses and contact lenses, differences between near- and farsightedness, and color blindness. After the visit, ask the school nurse to give students eye exams.

DEPTH PERCEPTION

MATERIALS
- ▲ none

Divide the class into groups of two. Ask students to stand arm's length apart, face their partners, and cover one eye. Have them extend the index finger of the free hand toward the partner's index finger so their fingers meet in the air. Have students try again if they missed. Then, ask students to repeat the experiment using both eyes. Explain that two eyes are needed to see depth.

MATERIALS

▲ touch objects (sandpaper, stuffed animals, rocks, fabric)

▲ smell objects (lemon, perfume, flowers, onion, potpourri)

▲ taste objects (pickles, raisins, salty crackers, apple slices)

▲ sound objects (bell, tambourine, alarm clock, timer)

▲ blindfolds

TRUST YOUR SENSES

Discuss with students what life would be like without sight. Set up stations for touch, smell, taste, and sound in the classroom. Pair students, designating one partner as "leader" and the other as "follower." Blindfold the followers and tell the leaders to hold their partners' hands. Send three or four pairs to a sense station. Have followers try to identify objects by feeling, smelling, tasting, and listening as they walk around the classroom to each sense station. Before leaders and followers trade places and repeat the activity, discuss observations followers had while "blind," such as needing to trust others, depending on other senses, or feeling afraid.

MATERIALS

▲ Eye Chart reproducible (page 41)

▲ stickers

YOU BE THE DOCTOR

HOME ACTIVITY

Send home the Eye Chart reproducible with students, and invite them to give eye exams to their family members. Ask "eye doctors" to post the chart on a wall (with permission) or prop it up on a chair. Tell them to have their "patients" stand back 20' (6 m) and cover one eye while reading the letters. Advise the eye doctors to give stickers to their patients. Ask eye doctors to write down the results and share them with the class.

EYE CHART

E

RB

PTD

SCF2

ZLWYH

ATQRNE

MPJGIOF

NEW YEAR'S DAY

January 1

New Year's Day is the beginning of the calendar year. Some people eat black-eyed peas for good luck and green cabbage for more money. Other traditions include parties, parades, football games, resolutions, and reflections on the past. Whatever the tradition, ring in the new year with pizzazz in your classroom.

LITERATURE LINKS

Emily Arrow Promises to Do Better This Year
by Patricia Reilly Giff

Happy New Year!
by Emery Bernhard

Happy New Year, Pooh!
by Kathleen Zoehfeld

We Celebrate New Year
by Bobbie Kalman

Where's Molly?
by Uli Waas

BABY NEW YEAR

Can You Match the Baby Face?

BABY NEW YEAR BULLETIN BOARD

Ask families to send in their children's baby pictures for a Baby New Year bulletin board. Be sure to bring your own picture. Cut out one construction-paper balloon for each student. Tape a baby picture to each balloon, and attach the balloons to a bulletin board. Staple a yarn piece to each balloon, and clip a clothespin to the end. Have students make "diapers" from envelopes. Instruct them to fold the top flap in, cut the bottom corners at an angle for leg holes, and decorate their "diapers." Invite students to write their names on the diapers and place them in a shoe box near the board. Challenge students to match diapers to baby pictures.

MATERIALS
- students' baby pictures
- scissors
- construction paper
- tape
- stapler
- yarn
- clothespins
- 3 ½" x 5 ½" (9 cm x 14 cm) envelopes
- crayons or markers
- shoe box

TWO-FACED MASKS

Tell students about the ancient Roman god Janus (for whom January is named). Janus was the guardian of doorways and had two faces, one for looking ahead to the future and one for looking back to the past. Give each student two paper plates. Invite students to draw and cut out two related masks, such as opposite feelings (happiness and sadness), paired images (sun and moon or Father Time and Baby New Year), or opposed story characters (Little Red Riding Hood and Wolf). Have students color and decorate their masks, cutting out holes for the eyes, nose, and mouth. Help them punch holes on either side of their two masks and thread yarn through the holes. Ask students to thread the masks together on one side, put on their masks, and tie the other sides together. Invite each student to wear and present the masks, explaining each side while shifting a face to the front.

GOOD, BETTER, BEST

According to superstition, the way you act and feel on New Year's Day will be the way you act and feel all year. To help students start off the year on the right foot, teach the following affirmative chants. Copy them onto sentence strips, and invite students to copy and illustrate one.

I feel good.
I feel fine.
I feel this way all the time.

Good, better, best.
Never let it rest.
Until your good gets better
And your better gets best.

Climb high.
Climb far.
Your goal, the sky.
Your aim, a star.

MATERIALS

▲ Glancing Back, Looking Forward reproducible (page 46)

▲ crayons or markers

GLANCING BACK, LOOKING FORWARD

With the start of the new year, many people spend time reflecting on the past. Invite students to think about the past school year. Give them the Glancing Back, Looking Forward reproducible and invite them to write and draw what they have done well and what they want to improve. For younger students, send the reproducible home for parent help. Invite students to share their work and display finished projects on a bulletin board titled *Glancing Back, Looking Forward.*

MATERIALS

▲ paper-towel tubes

▲ crayons or markers

▲ tape

▲ tissue paper

▲ writing paper

▲ drawing paper

▲ trinkets

▲ large can with lid

TIME CAPSULES

Have each student decorate a paper-towel tube and close off one end with taped-on tissue paper. Invite students to write lists of current favorites (animals, foods, books, colors, drinks, activities, holidays, movies, songs, sports, games, television shows, and friends). Ask them to draw self-portraits and write their names underneath. Have students roll their papers into a scroll and place them inside the tube. Invite students to add three or four trinkets, such as a class photo, a penny from the year, a piece of jewelry, or a toy. Then have students close the other end with tissue paper. Send the time capsules home or place them all in a large can (like a popcorn gift canister), and invite students to return in five years to open them as a group. Notify the local newspaper before the reunion.

TURN OVER A NEW LEAF

Start the new year by inviting students to set weekly goals. Challenge students to choose school-related goals, such as raising hands before talking, writing names on papers, keeping desks clean, and turning work in on time. Encourage students to choose new goals, rather than something they already do well. Have students complete a Reach for the Stars reproducible each week. At the end of each day, have students evaluate themselves. If they met their goals, place stickers on their charts for that day. As students reach a goal, invite them to draw or write it on the Turn Over a New Leaf reproducible, cut it out, and attach it to a bulletin board titled *Turn Over a New Leaf.*

MUSIC MAKERS

Making noise—from blowing horns to ringing bells—is a popular New Year's custom. Invite students to draw colorful New Year's Day scenes on construction paper. Have students place the drawings (scene side out) inside clear, empty tennis ball tubes and tape in place. Help students fill the tubes with rice or sand and secure the lids with tape. Invite your students to ring in the new year with their festive noisemakers.

GLANCING BACK, LOOKING FORWARD

Name _____

Over the past few _____

days, weeks, months

I did well at _____

_____

I also _____

I could improve _____

_____

To improve I will _____

_____

_____

January © 1997 Creative Teaching Press

REACH FOR THE STARS

MONDAY	TUESDAY	WEDNESDAY	THURSDAY	FRIDAY

This week, my goal is to _____

_____

_____

I will do my best and let you know how I'm doing. _____

(signed)

TURN OVER A NEW LEAF

January © 1997 Creative Teaching Press

SLURPY SOUP DAY

January is National Soup Month. Warm up an icy cold January day with a cup of soup. Read books about cooking and eating delicious soups. Your students will love these delicious activities!

LITERATURE LINKS

Chicken Soup with Rice by Maurice Sendak

Famous Seaweed Soup by Antoinette Truglio Martin

Growing Vegetable Soup by Lois Ehlert

Lentil Soup by Joe Lasker

Mouse Soup by Arnold Lobel

Stone Soup by Marcia Brown

Vegetable Soup by Jeanne Modesitt

SILLY SOUP

Make "hodgepodge" soup by mixing three or four different kinds of soup in a slow cooker. Ask your students to assist serving soup and crackers. After enjoying soup together, invite students to create their own silly soup recipes on the Soup Pot reproducible. Make a bulletin board by drawing a large soup can on butcher paper. Fold in the sides about an inch (2.5 cm). Staple the folded sides on the bulletin board so the can curves outward, creating a three-dimensional display. Title the bulletin board *Soup-er Work* and attach student recipes.

MATERIALS
▲ 3 or 4 cans of different soups
▲ slow cooker
▲ paper cups or bowls
▲ plastic spoons
▲ crackers
▲ Soup Pot reproducible (page 51)
▲ butcher paper
▲ markers
▲ stapler

SOUP SACK STORY

Read *Growing Vegetable Soup* aloud. Copy the reproducible, and make vegetable and bowl templates from tagboard. Have each student trace and cut out vegetables and a bowl from construction paper. Have students complete the following frame on each vegetable. *(Student's name) put in a (vegetable name).* Have each student write *(Student's name) put in a spoon and ate it all up! Yum!* and glue it to a plastic spoon. Have students glue their bowls to the front of paper lunch sacks and write *(Student's name) grew vegetable soup!* Invite students to read the sentence strips, place them in their soup sacks, and place their spoons in last.

SOUPY SOUNDS

Cut large bowls from construction paper using the bowl from the Vegetables reproducible as a pattern. Have students brainstorm vocabulary words that describe soup and print one word on each bowl. Put the word bowls, extra blank bowls, and a scoop of cereal in a resealable plastic bag. Place the bag in a learning center. Have students place cereal pieces on the bowls to make words.

SOUP POT

VEGETABLES

January © 1997 Creative Teaching Press

VEGETABLES

PEANUT DAY

January 5

America is nuts about peanuts, and we can thank George Washington Carver for making them such a popular food. Born on January 5, 1860, Carver created more than 300 products from peanuts, including soap, ink, face powder, and peanut soup! In a nutshell, peanut day should be a crack-up.

LITERATURE LINKS

From Peanuts to Peanut Butter
by Melvin Berger

Make Me a Peanut Butter Sandwich and a Glass of Milk
by Ken Robbins

Peanut Butter
by Arlene Erlbach

A Pocketful of Goobers: A Story about George Washington Carver
by Barbara Mitchell

A Weed Is a Flower: The Life of George Washington Carver
by Aliki

NUTS ABOUT MATH

Give each student a handful of peanuts to decorate as monkeys. Have students draw faces on the peanuts with black markers and glue on a string tail. Invite students to make palm trees and grass from torn construction paper and glue the decorations to a background. Have each student glue a few "monkeys" to the tree and a few monkeys to the grass. Have students write an addition sentence to match their paper, such as *5 monkeys on the tree + 2 monkeys on the grass = 7 monkeys.* Display student papers on a large palm tree cut from butcher paper hung on a door or wall titled *Monkey See, Monkey Do, Monkeys Add, So Can You!*

MATERIALS
▲ unshelled peanuts
▲ black markers
▲ glue
▲ string
▲ construction paper
▲ butcher paper

PLANTING PEANUTS

MATERIALS

▲ unshelled raw peanuts (not roasted)

▲ resealable plastic bag

▲ moist soil

▲ sharp pencils

▲ construction-paper peanut shapes

Invite each student to crack a peanut shell and place the peanut in a resealable plastic bag. Have each student add a scoop of moist soil, seal the bag, and poke a few air holes in the bag with a sharp pencil. Invite students to attach their bags to a bulletin board titled *Nuts about Peanuts.* Ask students to predict when their peanuts will sprout. (Germination usually takes about two weeks.) Have students record their predictions on construction-paper peanuts and attach them next to their bags. When the seeds begin to sprout, let students take their peanut plants home to plant outdoors.

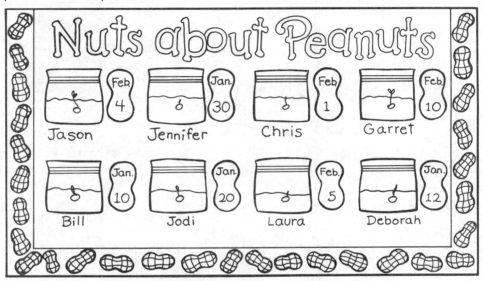

PEANUT PREDICTIONS

MATERIALS

▲ clear plastic jar

▲ unshelled peanuts

▲ construction-paper peanut shapes

Fill a clear jar with peanuts. Pass the jar around so students can study and estimate the number of peanuts in the jar. Remind students that each shell usually contains two peanuts. Have students record their estimates on peanut shapes. Ask student volunteers to shell and count the peanuts. Invite the student with the closest estimation to take the jar home and fill it with other objects for the class to estimate. Continue this fun estimation practice each week.

OLD-FASHIONED PEANUT BUTTER

MATERIALS

▲ Peanut Butter recipe (page 56)

▲ sentence strips

▲ pocket chart

▲ blender

▲ rubber spatula

▲ crackers

Use the Peanut Butter recipe to build sequencing and measurement skills. On individual sentence strips, write each recipe step. Place the strips in random order in a pocket chart. Assist students as they sequence the steps. Then start cooking!

PEANUT BUTTER

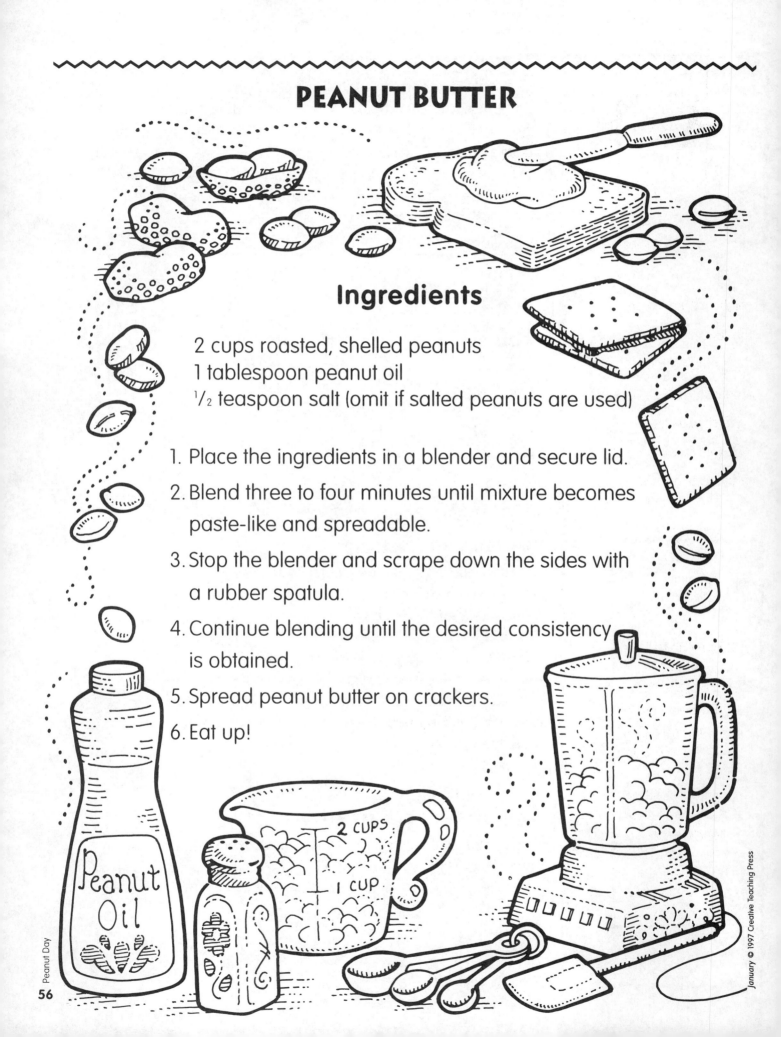

Ingredients

2 cups roasted, shelled peanuts
1 tablespoon peanut oil
$\frac{1}{2}$ teaspoon salt (omit if salted peanuts are used)

1. Place the ingredients in a blender and secure lid.

2. Blend three to four minutes until mixture becomes paste-like and spreadable.

3. Stop the blender and scrape down the sides with a rubber spatula.

4. Continue blending until the desired consistency is obtained.

5. Spread peanut butter on crackers.

6. Eat up!

January © 1997 Creative Teaching Press

BALLOON BLAST-OFF DAY

January 9

The first hot-air balloon flight in America occurred on January 9, 1793. Today, there are over 2,000 American sport balloonists. Watch your students take off with these fun balloon creations and experiments!

LITERATURE LINKS

Airplanes and Balloons
by Howard W. Kanetzke

The Big Balloon Race
by Eleanor Coerr

*The First Air Voyage
in the United States*
by Alexandra Wallner

*The Great Valentine's Day
Balloon Race*
by Adrienne Adams

Hot Air Henry
by Mary Calhoun

*Wings:
A Tale of Two Chickens*
by James Marshall

BALLOON BUDDIES

Help each student blow up a balloon and knot the end. Divide the class into pairs. Have one partner stand on a piece of construction paper, heels together, toes apart. Ask the other student to trace his or her partner's feet. Then, have students trade places and repeat the process. Invite students to draw shoes on their feet patterns and cut them out, keeping the shoes attached at the heels. Have them punch holes in the shoes and lace yarn through the holes for shoelaces. Have each student cut a 1" (2.5 cm) slit in the feet at the heels and insert the knotted end of the balloon into the slit so the balloon stands up. Invite students to decorate their balloons with crazy hair, silly faces, and other funny features using markers, yarn, and construction-paper scraps. Invite students to write stories about their goofy balloon buddies before they take the buddies home.

HOT AIR RISES

MATERIALS
▲ blow-dryer
▲ plastic garbage bag

Sit on the floor with a plastic garbage bag on your lap. Place the nozzle of a blow-dryer into the bag and carefully gather the bag around the nozzle. While holding tightly, turn the blow-dryer on high until the bag is completely filled. (The bag will quickly inflate and rise.) Turn the blow-dryer off so the plastic doesn't melt. Explain that heat makes the air in the bag expand. The heated air in the bag is lighter than the cooler surrounding air, making the bag rise just like a hot-air balloon!

BALLOON BAGS

MATERIALS
▲ pictures of hot-air balloons
▲ paper lunch sacks
▲ crayons or markers
▲ newspaper
▲ yarn
▲ hole punch
▲ paper cups

After showing students pictures of hot-air balloons, invite them to decorate paper lunch sacks to create their own unique balloon designs. Have students stuff crumpled newspaper inside the sacks and tie the open end closed with yarn. Have students hole-punch opposite sides of paper-cup "baskets" and paper-bag "balloons." Ask them to thread yarn through the holes to tie the balloons to the baskets. Hang the hot-air balloons from the ceiling for a colorful classroom display.

FAIRY TALE DAY

January 12

Charles Perrault was born on January 12, 1628, in France, and is best known for writing *The Tales of Mother Goose*, a book of fairy tales. Engage your students in a fun fairy tale fantasy day!

LITERATURE LINKS

Cinderella by Charles Perrault

Little Red Riding Hood by Charles Perrault

Paper Bag Princess by Robert Munsch

Perrault's Fairy Tales by Charles Perrault

Prince Cinders by Babette Cole

Puss in Boots by Charles Perrault

Sleeping Beauty by Charles Perrault

Tom Thumb by Charles Perrault

ROYAL PARTY

Have students pretend they are princes and princesses planning a royal party. Give students one Royal Invitation reproducible each, and ask them to complete the invitation for a real or imaginary friend. Have them fold it on the solid vertical line and then on the dotted horizontal line. Have students draw stamps and address the envelopes. Then, have a real royal party! Engage students in various "royal" activities, such as wearing royal blue or choosing a friend to "knight" for doing something great. For a royal party game, first write royal and not-so-royal fairy tale characters' names on index cards and tape one to each student's back. Then have students ask each other yes-or-no questions to discover which characters they are. Close the day by reading a royal fairy tale such as *Cinderella*.

MATERIALS
- ▲ Royal Invitation reproducible (page 61)
- ▲ crayons or markers
- ▲ index cards
- ▲ tape
- ▲ fairy tale

PERSONALITY PORTRAYALS

Divide the class into groups. Invite each group to select a fairy tale character and illustrate it on butcher paper using paint. While pictures dry, brainstorm as a class and write on index cards or sentence strips words that describe each character. After pictures dry, have students cut them out and outline them with black marker. Hang them on a bulletin board, and invite students to surround each character with its describing words.

FAIRY TALE FLIP-FLAP BOOKS

Have students fold construction paper in half, lengthwise. Then have students fold the paper in half, and then in half again. Ask students to open and cut the top flap on the fold lines to the center fold as shown. Have students write *main character, setting, problem,* and *solution* on the front flaps. Discuss these elements, and invite students to choose a fairy tale and illustrate it under the flaps. Ask students to share their flip books with the class.

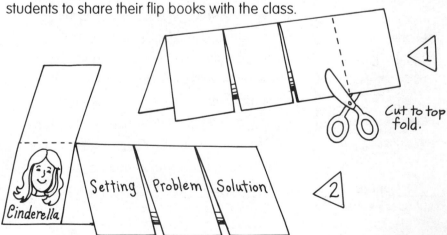

A ROYAL INVITATION

❦ A Royal Invitation ❦

Hear Ye! Hear Ye! Hear Ye!

is cordially invited to

a _____

on _____

at _____

You can look forward to eating _____

and listening and dancing to _____ .

Signed, _____

To: _____
_____
_____

MARTIN LUTHER KING, JR., DAY

Third Monday in January

This national holiday celebrates the life and work of Dr. Martin Luther King, Jr., who was born on January 15, 1929. Dr. King believed in nonviolence and spent his life working for justice and equality for all people.

LITERATURE LINKS

Martin Luther King Day
by Linda Lowery

*Martin Luther King, Jr.:
A Picture Story*
by Margaret Boone-Jones

Meet Martin Luther King, Jr.
by James T. De Kay

Peace Begins with You
by Katherine Scholes

People by Peter Spier

*A Picture Book of
Martin Luther King, Jr.*
by David A. Adler

ON-THE-RIGHT-TRACK BULLETIN BOARD

Copy the Train pattern onto several sheets of construction paper and cut out the trains. Print positive behavior sentences such as *I am kind, I share, I listen, I cooperate with others,* or *I am friendly* on each train car. Attach train cars to a bulletin board titled *On the Right Track* by stapling three sides and leaving the top open. Tape student photos to craft sticks. Each morning, have students choose a character trait from the board that they would like to focus on during the day. Have students place their sticks in the chosen cars. At the end of the day, ask students to remove their sticks and tell how they did.

MATERIALS
▲ Train reproducible (page 66)
▲ various colors of construction paper
▲ scissors
▲ stapler
▲ tape
▲ student photographs
▲ craft sticks

RED RIBBON/YELLOW RIBBON

One way to understand prejudice is to experience it. Play this game to demonstrate how some people are treated with prejudice. Divide the class into two groups. Give one group red ribbons and the other yellow ribbons. Have students tie the ribbons to their arms. During class, only call on students with red ribbons. Allow the red group to have free time, but give an assignment to the yellow group. Finally, excuse the red group to recess early and the yellow group late. When students return from recess, discuss how it felt for the yellow group to be ignored and mistreated and for the red group to get preferential treatment. Ask the red group if they found themselves gloating and feeling more important than the yellow group. Relate this activity to how different groups of people are sometimes treated.

PEACE BEGINS WITH ME

Have students draw a large peace sign and write a label in each section: *In class, At home, In my neighborhood,* and *On the playground.* Invite students to write or draw in each section how they can create peace by avoiding conflict and solving problems positively. Ask students to cut out the peace signs and attach them to a bulletin board titled *Peace Begins with Me.*

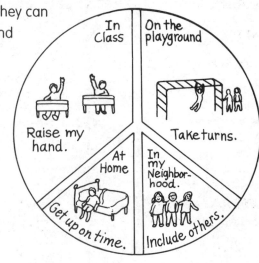

PEACEMAKERS BULLETIN BOARD

Make a bulletin board titled *Peacemakers Solve Problems Peacefully.* Cut out several doves from the reproducible. When students solve a problem peacefully, invite them to illustrate or write on a dove how they solved the problem. Attach the doves to the bulletin board. Reward the class with Dove® ice-cream bars when the board is full.

I-HAVE-A-DREAM MOBILE

MATERIALS
▲ scissors
▲ drawing paper
▲ hole punch
▲ string
▲ hanger
▲ tape

Have students cut out five clouds from drawing paper. Invite students to draw on each cloud a dream they have for their family, school, community, country, or world. Have students write (or dictate to be written) a caption under each drawing. Ask students to write on the back of each cloud (or dictate) one thing they can do to make their dreams reality. Have students hole-punch the top of their clouds, tie a string to each cloud, and hang the clouds from a hanger. Have students cut out and attach with tape two larger clouds to cover each side of the hanger and then write *I Have a Dream* on the front.

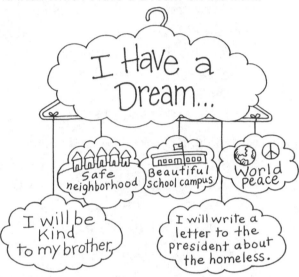

WHO I AM MAKES A DIFFERENCE

MATERIALS
▲ Who I Am Makes a Difference reproducible (page 67)
▲ colored paper
▲ scissors
▲ crayons or markers
▲ safety pins

Cut out one Who I Am Makes a Difference reproducible badge from colored paper for each student. Write on the badge one way the student makes a difference. Pin a badge on each student. Ask students to discuss people they know personally and admire. Have students choose one person each to honor with a "Who I Am Makes a Difference" badge. Ask students to brainstorm that person's positive attributes. Have students list or draw on the badge, how that person makes a difference. Invite each student to pin the badge on the person they admire and give two blank badges to that person to give to someone who makes a difference in his or her life. The next recipient will have one extra badge to give away. Ask students to share how their badges made a difference.

UNITED AND UNIQUE

Cut a string of large butcher-paper paper dolls connected at the hands, one doll per student. Invite each student to decorate a doll using paint and craft materials. Have students write their names in the center of their dolls. Have students write or dictate something special about themselves on sentence strips and glue the strips to the bottom of their dolls. Discuss with students how they are united and unique. Hang the chain from a string across the ceiling.

OUR HELPING HANDS

Read aloud or play a tape of "I Have a Dream." Have each student trace one hand on construction paper. Ask students to write on the smallest finger the name of an organization or group they want to help. Have them write on each of the next three fingers ways they can help. Have students write their names on the thumb and draw on the palm a picture of themselves being helpful. Arrange the hands on a bulletin board titled *Our Helping Hands.* As an extension, let students participate in a service project, such as helping in a retirement home, homeless shelter, children's hospital, or soup kitchen, so all students can lend their helping hands!

Martin Luther King, Jr., Day

TRAIN

January © 1997 Creative Teaching Press

DOVE

WHO I AM MAKES A DIFFERENCE

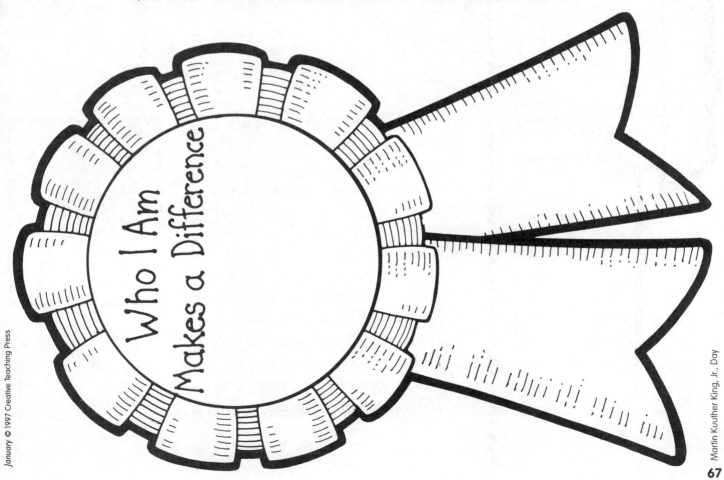

Who I Am Makes a Difference

Martin Kuuther King, Jr., Day

CLEAN DESK DAY

You can celebrate
National Clean Off Your
Desk Day *every* Monday!
These neat activities help
make a tidy classroom.

LITERATURE LINKS

Eeps, Creeps, It's My Room
by Martha Whitmore Hickman

*I Meant to Clean
My Room Today*
by Miriam Nerlove

I Need to Clean My Room,
CTP Learn to Read Series

Mooch the Messy
by Marjorie Weinman Sharmat

Never Spit on Your Shoes
by Denys Cazet

BETTER NOW THAN LATER

Read aloud "Sarah Cynthia Sylvia Stout
Would Not Take the Garbage Out." Discuss
the word *procrastinate* and ask students
what they do to procrastinate when they
should be cleaning their rooms, doing
homework, or doing chores around the
house. Have students write on milk cartons,
old envelopes, and other "garbage" ways
they procrastinate. Attach the garbage on a
bulletin board display titled *Sarah Cynthia
Sylvia Stout Threw Her Procrastinations Out!*
Have a ceremony during which students can
throw out their procrastinations.

MATERIALS

▲ "Sarah Cynthia Sylvia
Stout Would Not Take
the Garbage Out" from
*Where the Sidewalk
Ends* by Shel Silverstein

▲ markers

▲ "garbage" (milk
cartons, labels,
old envelopes)

WHITE-GLOVE TEST

Give each student a paper grocery bag labeled *Too Much Stuff.* Have students empty their desks or cubbies and put in their bags items that do not belong in their desks. Ask students to neatly arrange their desks or cubbies and wipe off their desks with a paper towel. To help them manage their time, give students a two-minute warning before asking them to finish. Remind students to bring their sacks home. Invite a student to volunteer as "desk inspector." Give the inspector a white glove to wear while he or she administers a white-glove test. Have the inspector reward clean-desk keepers with treats.

CLEAN-SHAVEN DESKS

Spray a dab of shaving cream on each student's desktop. Invite students to finger-paint with the shaving cream to clean their desks. The room will smell fresh, desks will be clean, and children will have fun. Ask other teachers if your students can clean their tables. Back in class, discuss the benefits of hard work and helping others.

HEY, DESK, HOW DO YOU FEEL?

Have students look inside their desks or cubbies and think about how the areas look. Ask students to decorate the Desk reproducible to resemble their desks or cubbies. Invite each student to imagine how the desk or cubby feels and write what it would say to its owner. Encourage students to keep their desks smiling by keeping their desks tidy!

Name_____

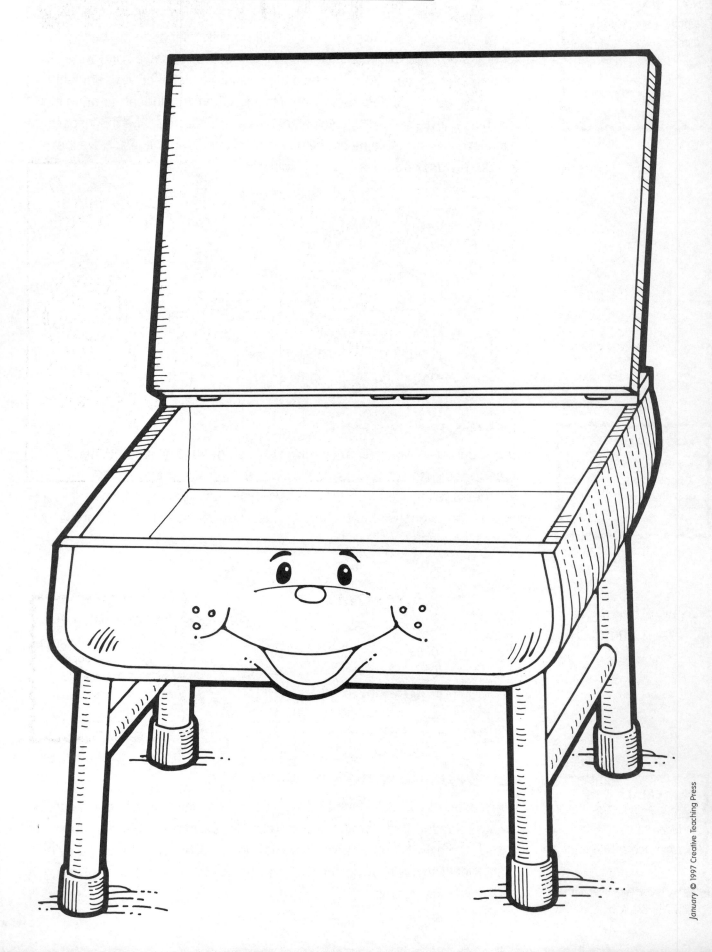

January © 1997 Creative Teaching Press

DO NOTHING DAY

January 16

National Do Nothing Day is an actual day created by a journalist "to provide Americans with one national day when they can just sit without celebrating, observing, or honoring anything." Students will love the opportunity to do just that. It is harder than they might expect!

LITERATURE LINKS

Be a Perfect Person in Just Three Days! by Stephen Manes

Bored, Nothing to Do! by Peter Spier

The Cat in the Hat by Dr. Seuss

The House at Pooh Corner by A.A. Milne

My Mom Hates Me in January by Judy Delton

Nothing Ever Happens on My Block by Ellen Raskin

WE'RE NOT BORED

Cut out large raindrops from construction paper. Read *The Cat in the Hat* aloud. Have students list the activities the story characters did during the rainy day when they could not go outside to play. Discuss productive things to do, instead of watching TV or playing video games, when bored. Have students write their ideas on the construction-paper raindrops. Display raindrops on a bulletin board titled *We're Not Bored!*

MATERIALS
▲ scissors
▲ construction paper
▲ *The Cat in the Hat* by Dr. Seuss

BE A PERFECT PERSON

In an effort to be perfect, the main character in *Be a Perfect Person in Just Three Days!* follows some strange advice. Share the book with students, and have them experiment with the advice. First, have each student tie yarn around a piece of broccoli to wear as a necklace. Ask students to describe how hanging broccoli around their necks might give them courage. Then, have students follow the other advice from the book by sitting silently and thinking for five minutes while sipping weak tea. Ask them to write or draw everything they thought about while they sipped tea. Have a discussion about the advantages and disadvantages of being a "perfect" person.

GONE FISHIN'

Have students cut construction-paper fish and brainstorm productive free-time classroom activities. Invite students to write an activity on each fish and poke a paper clip through the fish's mouth. Have students place the fish in a fishbowl. Tie string to a stick or ruler and attach a magnet for a "fishing pole." When students have nothing to do, have them toss out the fishing pole and "go fishing" for activities.

WINNIE-THE-POOH DAY

January 18

A. A. Milne, born on January 18, 1882, wrote verses and stories for his son, Christopher Robin. Have your class join Christopher Robin and his friends, Pooh, Piglet, Kanga, Roo, Eeyore, Owl, Rabbit, and Tigger on a blustery day in the Hundred Acre Wood!

LITERATURE LINKS

The House at Pooh Corner by A. A. Milne

Now We Are Six by A. A. Milne

The Pooh Cook Book by Virginia H. Ellison

The Teddy Bears' Picnic by Jimmy Kennedy

When We Were Very Young by A. A. Milne

Winnie-the-Pooh by A. A. Milne

TEDDY BEAR TEA PARTY

Invite students to bring their teddy bears to class for a teddy bear tea party. Make "Pooh Tea" (see recipe below) and serve it with a special snack. Invite students to record the events of the tea party on copies of the Teddy Bear reproducible and cut them out. Bind into a class teddy bear book.

Pooh Tea
1. Heat water and mint leaves.
2. Add lemonade.
3. Stir in honey.

MATERIALS
▲ Pooh Tea (hot water, mint leaves, lemonade, honey)
▲ teapot
▲ spoon
▲ cups
▲ snacks (scones, cookies, cucumber sandwiches)
▲ Teddy Bear reproducible (page 75)
▲ scissors
▲ bookbinding materials

MATERIALS

▲ *Now We Are Six*
  by A. A. Milne
▲ sentence strips
▲ drawing paper
▲ crayons or markers
▲ bookbinding
  materials

NOW WE ARE SIX

Read *Now We Are Six* to your class. On sentence strips, write the frames *When I was one, _____. When I was two, _____. When I was three, _____. When I was four, _____. When I was five, _____. Now that I am six, _____.* Have students copy, complete with accomplishments from each year, and illustrate the frames on separate sheets of paper. Bind into individual books.

MATERIALS

▲ *The House at Pooh Corner* by A.A. Milne
▲ 12" x 18"
  (30.5 cm x 46 cm)
  construction paper
▲ crayons or markers
▲ drawing paper
▲ scissors
▲ glue

POOH-CORNER MAP

Share "In Which Tigger Is Unbounced" from *The House at Pooh Corner.* Discuss how Pooh and his friends often get lost. To have students help Pooh and his friends find their way, ask each student to draw a map on construction paper that includes Pooh Corner; the forest; the Six Pine Trees; Eeyore's lost house; Tigger's, Kanga and Roo's, and Christopher Robin's houses; Rabbit's house; and Owl's house in the Hundred Acre Wood. Have students draw characters from the story on separate drawing paper, cut them out, and glue them onto their maps.

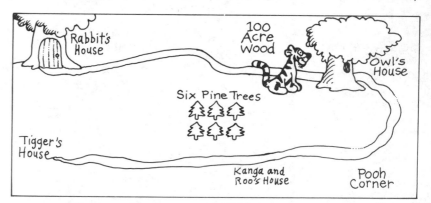

TEDDY BEAR JOURNAL PACK

Give students opportunities to take a teddy bear home for a weekend and write about their experiences with it. Invite students to share their experiences with the class each Monday. To model, take the bear home first and write a rich account of what you did together. Send the bear and journal home with a different student each weekend.

TEDDY BEAR

HAT DAY

January 20

Almost everyone loves wearing a hat! Hat Day celebrates the many hats worn throughout the world. Whether it is a beret, sombrero, derby, baseball cap, ten-gallon hat, or top hat, have students wear and create their favorite chapeau on this festive day. Hats off to the students who create the wackiest hats!

LITERATURE LINKS

Caps for Sale
by Esphyr Slobodkina

The 500 Hats of Bartholomew Cubbins by Dr. Seuss

Hats, Hats, Hats
by Ann Morris

Jennie's Hat
by Ezra Jack Keats

Martin's Hats by Joan W. Blos

Mister Momboo's Hat
by Ralph Leemis

Next Time, Take Care
by Ann Lindbergh

HAT PARTY

Give each student a hat and a variety of art supplies. Have students write their names inside their hats. Set a timer to give students two minutes to decorate their hats. Have each student pass the hat to the person on the left to decorate it for two minutes. Have students pass and decorate the hats until they are returned to their original owners.

MATERIALS

▲ inexpensive party hats
▲ art supplies (feathers, sequins, fabric scraps, glitter)
▲ glue
▲ markers
▲ timer

HATS, HATS, HATS

MATERIALS

▲ 2 ½' (76 cm) butcher paper squares
▲ masking tape
▲ paint/paintbrushes
▲ art supplies (sequins, feathers, glitter)

Divide the class into pairs. Have one partner center the butcher paper on the other's head and mold the paper around it. Instruct the hatmaker to wrap the base of the crown with masking tape to hold the shape. Then have the hatmaker roll and bunch the paper around the crown to form a brim. Invite partners to trade places and make another hat and then let them decorate their hats with paint and other art supplies.

A FEATHER IN YOUR CAP

MATERIALS

▲ 12" x 18" (30.5 cm x 46 cm) construction paper
▲ tape
▲ feathers

Introduce this activity by discussing the phrase "That's a feather in your cap." Have students fold construction paper in half and then fold the top two corners down from the fold so they meet in the center. Have them fold up the "brim" on each side and tuck two corners into the back to secure the brim. Have each student tape a feather to the hat and print his or her name on it. Invite students to pass their hats around the classroom. Ask each student to write on each hat a positive comment about the owner.

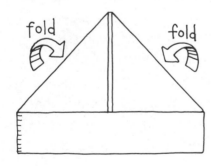

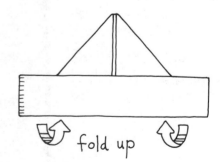

GIVE-A-HUG DAY

Everyone loves a hug!
National Hugging Day
is celebrated on
January 21. Invite
students to make
hug cards or coupons,
or play a hug game
on this lovable day.
How about a hug?

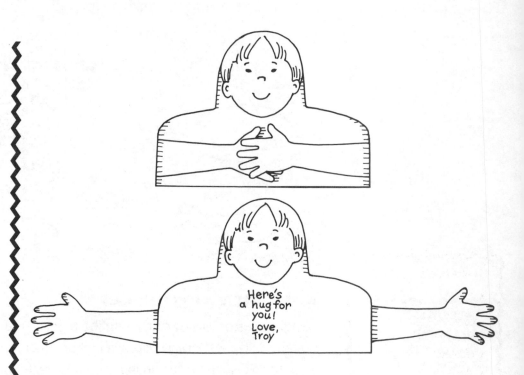

LITERATURE LINKS

Bear Hugs
by Kathleen Hague

A Book of Hugs
by Dave Ross

Guess How Much I Love You
by Sam McBratney

"Hug O War" from
Where the Sidewalk Ends
by Shel Silverstein

Hugs, Smiles, and Kisses
by Nancy Vittorini, Joan
Wilson, and Ellen Duris

Love You Forever
by Robert Munsch

HUG CARDS

Draw an outline for each student's head
and shoulders on construction paper.
Invite students to draw self-portraits on
their patterns and cut them out. Ask
students to trace around their hands and
arms (up to their elbows) on construction
paper and cut them out. Have students
glue the arm cutouts to the back of the
construction paper at the elbow and fold
them across the bottom of the page.
Invite students to write *Here's a hug
for you!* under the arms and give their
surprise hug to someone special.

MATERIALS
▲ construction paper
▲ crayons or markers
▲ scissors
▲ glue

HUG CHAIN

Invite students to spread out in a large play area. Call out a number between three and ten. Challenge children to form groups of the number called. When they have the right number, have them link arms and sit down. The first seated group is the winner. For a greater challenge, call out a math equation such as *seven minus three.* In this case, the first group of four to link arms and sit down wins.

HUG COUPONS

Give students ten construction-paper strips each, and have them write *A hug for _____ because _____* on each strip. Ask students to illustrate their coupon booklets and staple them together. Invite students to complete their hug coupons and pass them out to their family members.

THINGS THAT HUG

Read *Hugs, Smiles, and Kisses* aloud. Have students list other items that "hug," such as slippers that hug feet after a bath or bandages that hug elbows after a fall. On sentence strips, write the frame _____ hugs _____ when _____. Invite students to copy, complete, and illustrate the frame on drawing paper. For example, <u>A fuzzy towel</u> hugs <u>me</u> when <u>I get out of the pool</u>, <u>A scarf</u> hugs <u>my neck</u> when <u>it's cold outside</u>, or <u>A hot dog bun</u> hugs <u>a hot dog</u> when <u>there's a barbecue.</u> Bind pages into a class book titled *Hugs.*

BUTTON DAY

Buttons come in all shapes and sizes—small, big, round, square, star, and moon. Colorful buttons make ideal math manipulatives for sorting, counting, or patterning. Chilly January is a perfect time to "button up" with buttons!

LITERATURE LINKS

The Button Box
by Margaret Reid

Buttons Buttons,
CTP Learn to Read Series

Elephant Buttons
by Noriko Ueno

Frog and Toad Are Friends
by Arnold Lobel

I Spy by Jean Marzollo

Large As Life by Julia Finzel

My Cat Likes to Hide in Boxes
by Eve Sutton

THAT'S NOT MY BUTTON!

Read "A Lost Button" aloud, and invite students to recreate the story in mini-books. Give each student three or four different buttons. Have students copy the sentences *I've lost my button. Please help me find it* on drawing paper. Ask each student to choose a "lost" button and set it aside. Have each student copy on drawing paper and complete the frames *That's not my button! That button is _____. My button was _____,* using descriptive words for the buttons. For example, *That's not my button! That button is round. My button is square.* Invite students to glue matching buttons on their papers. Have them complete the frame on separate sheets of paper and glue on the rest of their buttons, one per page, to continue their stories. Ask students to glue on the last page their "lost" button and write *Here's my button! It's right where I left it.* Invite students to illustrate their pages. Staple each student's book inside a construction-paper cover.

MATERIALS
▲ "A Lost Button" from *Frog and Toad Are Friends* by Arnold Lobel
▲ buttons
▲ drawing paper
▲ glue
▲ crayons or markers
▲ construction paper
▲ stapler

That's not my button!
That button is round.
My button was square.

GUESS MY BUTTON

MATERIALS
▲ buttons

Button characteristics provide a perfect opportunity to introduce adjectives. Explain that color, number, shape, and size words are describing words. Have students brainstorm describing words for different buttons as you hold the buttons up and write the words on the chalkboard. Have pairs of students place several buttons on a tabletop. Ask one student to secretly choose a button while his or her partner tries to guess by asking descriptive yes-or-no questions such as *Is it shiny? Is it small? Does it have four holes?* Have the guesser remove buttons that do not match the descriptive words until he or she guesses correctly.

BUTTON DAY

MATERIALS
▲ camera
▲ glue
▲ construction paper
▲ bookbinding materials

Invite students to participate in Button Day, on which everyone wears as many buttons as they can. At home, students can sew or glue extra buttons on old clothes or wear clothes with lots of buttons. Take a photograph of each student, glue it to construction paper, and under each picture, write how many buttons the student wore. For example, *Chris is wearing seven buttons on her shirt and three buttons on her pants. Chris has ten buttons.* Compile the pages into a class book.

Wyatt is wearing 10 buttons.

Wyatt is wearing 8 buttons on his shirt and 2 buttons on his pants.

BUTTON BAG

MATERIALS
▲ needle and thread or glue
▲ buttons
▲ cloth bag
▲ puffy paint or fabric markers
▲ *Buttons Buttons*, CTP Learn to Read Series
▲ plastic jar with lid

HOME ACTIVITY

Sew or glue colorful buttons to the outside of a cloth bag and use puffy paint or fabric markers to label the bag *Button Bag.* Place a copy of *Buttons Buttons* in the bag for students to read with family members. Also include a plastic jar of buttons and simple directions that ask students to estimate the number of buttons in the jar; count the buttons by fives and tens; pattern and sort buttons by size, color, shape, and number of holes; and create number problems.

AUSTRALIA DAY

Australia is the smallest continent and the only continent that is also a country. January 26, 1788, marks the anniversary of Australia's first British settlement. Australia is sometimes called the land "down under." Enchant students with tales from this exotic land of koalas, kangaroos, and kookaburras!

LITERATURE LINKS

AUSSIE ANIMAL ANTICS

Because Australia is a continent unattached to any other landmass, many of its animals are unique and live nowhere else in the world. Read aloud *ABC of Australian Animals*. Have students dictate one fact about each animal in the book and record the facts on chart paper. Invite students to follow these directions to make Australian animal quadraramas:

1. Fold down the top-right corner of one construction-paper square to meet the lower-left corner. Unfold, and repeat with the opposite corner.

2. Open, and cut on one fold line from the corner to the center of the square.

3. Draw a background scene on the top half of the square above the cut.

4. Overlap the two bottom triangles and glue them in place.

5. Make three more triaramas, and staple them together to form a quadrarama.

6. Decorate the sections to depict habitats of different Australian animals. Add text to each quadrant using the recorded facts.

7. Draw, cut out, and glue Australian animals to your quadrarama.

MATERIALS
- ▲ *ABC of Australian Animals* by Steve Parish
- ▲ chart paper
- ▲ 9" (23 cm) construction-paper squares
- ▲ scissors
- ▲ crayons or markers
- ▲ glue
- ▲ stapler

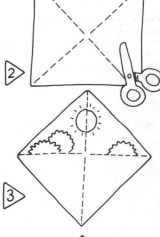

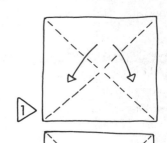

EIGHTH WONDER OF THE WORLD

MATERIALS

▲ *Great Barrier Reef* by Maura Gouck

▲ tempera paint/ paintbrushes

▲ butcher paper

▲ drawing paper

▲ black marker

▲ scissors

▲ glue

▲ fish-shaped blank books

▲ yarn

The Great Barrier Reef of Australia is the longest coral reef in the world. Read *Great Barrier Reef* aloud, and invite students to paint a Great Barrier Reef mural on butcher paper. Have each student choose one animal that makes the reef its home and paint it on drawing paper. When their drawings are dry, have students outline animals with black marker, cut them out, and glue them to the mural. Have each student create a small fish-shaped fact booklet about his or her animal and attach the booklet to the mural with yarn. Invite classmates to read about the animals and locate them on the mural.

WISH YOU WERE HERE

MATERIALS

▲ drawing paper

▲ crayons or markers

Have students fold a sheet of paper into thirds as the first step in creating an Australian travel guide. Invite students to design the cover and have them add an Australian map and flag. Have students illustrate the inside to advertise or highlight Australian sights, such as the Sydney Opera House, the Great Barrier Reef, Uluru (Ayer's Rock), the penguin parade in Victoria, kangaroos in Lone Pine, or koalas in the bush.

WHINGDING-DILLY DAY

Whingdingdilly is the name of a creature created by renowned children's author and illustrator Bill Peet, born on January 29, 1915. Before writing children's books, Peet worked for Walt Disney for 27 years as an illustrator on films, including *101 Dalmatians*.

LITERATURE LINKS

Books by Bill Peet

The Ant and the Elephant
Big Bad Bruce
Chester the Worldly Pig
Cock-A-Doodle Dudley
Cowardly Clyde
Encore for Eleanor
Huge Harold
Jennifer and Josephine
No Such Things
Whingdingdilly
The Wump World

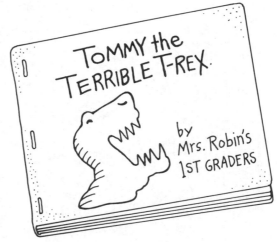

SILLY STORIES

Read some of Bill Peet's stories to your students and engage them in the following writing activities.

▲ *Cowardly Clyde* is about a horse who fears fighting a dragon with his master, Sir Galvant. Ask students what frightens them. Have them choose an animal to attribute that same fear to. Have students write a story about their new character and how it faces its fears.

▲ *Big Bad Bruce* is about a big, mean bear who picks on smaller animals in the forest until a witch casts a spell on him that shrinks him to the size of a squirrel. Invite the class to create a story about a creature that is unkind. However, have students alter the ending in this story so the creature learns to change its behavior. Write the story on chart paper, and invite students to work in small groups to illustrate parts of the story. Bind the pages into a class book.

MATERIALS
▲ *Cowardly Clyde* by Bill Peet
▲ writing paper
▲ construction paper
▲ bookbinding materials
▲ *Big Bad Bruce* by Bill Peet
▲ chart paper
▲ crayons or markers

RHYMING WHEEL OF FORTUNE

MATERIALS
▲ index cards
▲ pocket chart
▲ markers

Bill Peet's books contain lots of rhyming words. Write each letter of a rhyming word on a separate index card. Place the cards facedown in a pocket chart. Divide the class into two groups. Ask a volunteer to guess one of the letters in the chart. If the student guesses correctly, flip the card over to reveal the letter and ask another student from the group to guess a letter. When a student guesses incorrectly, the other group gets a turn to guess a letter. When a student guesses the word correctly, invite him or her to turn over the remaining letters. Challenge each group to name words that rhyme with the revealed word before you set up a new word.

KINDNESS COUNTS

MATERIALS
▲ *The Ant and the Elephant* by Bill Peet
▲ Kindness Counts reproducible (page 86)

The Ant and the Elephant shows the difference between animals who act kindly and animals who are rude. Read the story aloud to the class. Invite students to act out the story while you read. For added fun, stop the "play" at any time by calling *Freeze!* Have students freeze their positions, and choose new students to take their positions before calling *Action!* As a follow-up, send home the Kindness Counts reproducible for parents to complete. Ask parents to record ways their children are kind, helpful, patient, or forgiving during the week. The following week, invite students to share the ways their kindness counted.

Name _____

~~~~~~

KINDNESS COUNTS

This is how my child was kind, patient, helpful, and forgiving.

Monday

_____

_____

Tuesday

_____

_____

Wednesday

_____

_____

Thursday

_____

_____

Friday

_____

_____

PURPLE COW DAY

January 30

Purple Cow Day is
a silly way to
celebrate the birthday
of Gelette Burgess, who
wrote the popular verse:

I never saw a purple cow.

I never hope to see one.

But I can tell you, anyhow,

I'd rather see than be one!

LITERATURE LINKS

*Ed Emberley's Big Purple
Drawing Book*
by Ed Emberley

Harold and the Purple Crayon
by Crockett Johnson

I Love You the Purplest
by Barbara M. Joosse

If . . . by Sarah Perry

Lilly's Purple Plastic Purse
by Kevin Henkes

No Such Things
by Bill Peet

*Princess Prunella and the
Purple Peanut*
by Margaret Atwood

I never saw a *fuzzy green ear*.
I hope to never see one.
But I can tell you,
with a heart sincere,
I'd rather see than be one!

I'D RATHER SEE THAN BE ONE!

On sentence strips, write the frame *I never
saw a _____. I never hope to see one.
But I can tell you, _____, I'd rather see
than be one!* Have students copy and
complete the frame with their own creative
ideas. For example, *I never saw a spotted
pink slug. I never hope to see one. But I can
tell you, with a shrug, I'd rather see than be
one!* Invite students to illustrate and share
their verses.

MATERIALS
▲ sentence strips
▲ drawing paper
▲ crayons or markers

PURPLE COW SHAKES

Make a kooky purple drink on this wacky purple day. Give each student a cup with a scoop of vanilla ice cream or frozen yogurt in it and a spoon. Pour grape juice over the ice cream and serve. Invite students to make toasts to all the purple things they've ever seen and enjoy their purple "cow shakes."

IMAGINARY CREATURES

Purple cows are imaginary creatures created by Gelette Burgess. Invite students to cut out and glue different parts of magazine pictures together on construction paper to create their own imaginary creatures. Have students cut construction-paper frames and glue them below their creatures. Ask students to record their crazy creatures' names on the frame. Display on a bulletin board titled *Crazy Creatures!*

by Tyler

Wacka-Wookie-Bird

I LOVE YOU THE PURPLEST

Read aloud *I Love You the Purplest*. Discuss what the title might mean. Ask students to think of what or whom they love the purplest, reddest, or bluest. On sentence strips, write the frame *I love _____ the reddest. I love _____ the yellowest. I love _____ the bluest. I love _____ the greenest. I love _____ the orangest. I love _____ the pinkest. I love _____ the brownest. But I love _____ the purplest!* Have students copy, complete, and illustrate each sentence on color-coordinated construction paper. Bind individual books with construction-paper covers.

JANUARY

SUNDAY	MONDAY	TUESDAY	WEDNESDAY	THURSDAY	FRIDAY	SATURDAY

January © 1997 Creative Teaching Press

Snowflake Border

_____

_____

_____

_____

_____

_____

_____

_____

_____

_____

January News

January © 1997 Creative Teaching Press